Tomás Rivera

NUEVA ESPERANZA
ACADEMY CHARTER HIGH SCHOOL LIBRARY
Philadelphia, PA 19140

The Searchers: Collected Poetry

Edited by Julián Olivares

D1714238

Arte Publico Press
Houston
Texas
1990

The publication of this volume is made possible through grants from the Texas Commission on the Arts and the National Endowment for the Arts, a federal agency.

Arte Publico Press
University of Houston
Houston, Texas 77204-2090

Rivera, Tomás 1935–1984
    The Searchers: collected poetry / Tomás Rivera: edited by Julián Olivares
        p.   cm.
    English and Spanish
    ISBN 1-55885-018-X
    I. Olivares, Julián, 1941–   II. Title
PQ7079.2.R5A6 1990
861–dc20   90-191
                                                  CIP

The paper used in this publication meets the minimum requirements of the American National Standard for Permanence of Paper for Printed Library Materials Z39.48-1984. ∞

Copyright ©1990 Concepción Rivera
Printed in the United States of America

En memoria de Tomás
y para nuestros hijos:
Javier, Iracema e Ileana.

Concha Rivera

Contents

Tomás Rivera: Poet

When Tomás Rivera died in 1984, my regret and loss were deep and complex—too much so for words, I thought. As I read this collection, containing the volume of Tomás' poems entitled *Always and Other Poems* which I edited and published in 1973, I find he wrote what I feel. True, I was his editor, but that role was only the natural result of a meeting of two people who recognized their mutual love of the common experience of humanity. Neither of us thought that *common* meant without dignity or undeserving of celebration. *Common* is what we share: life, love, work and death. In the "Overalls" Tomás wrote of his own loss, an unending emptiness brought by death. Now he knows all any of us will ever know about death.

It is early spring in 1973, and I have been out in the country cutting wood, hard oak. As I cut, my mind goes to another task, the shaping of a volume of poetry—*Always and Other Poems*. Late afternoon, still in workboots and jeans, I stop at Tomás' office to talk about the poems. Tomás comes out of his office to put his arm around my shoulder and ask if I want a cup of coffee. I still hear him and see him, feel the strong hand gripping mine. Yet he could be hurt, where he was most sure:

> Frank, yesterday I was talking with these students about what is Chicano literature and what Chicano means. This young girl said to me: "You're standing up there in your coat and tie, with your house and job, you don't know what Chicano means." So I told her: "You're telling me that I was a migrant worker for twenty years and I don't know what Chicano means!"

To read the fine poem "The Searchers" is to understand why Tomás was angry. But as he told me about the students coming to talk, the anger went. He knew them, their anger and their love, as he said in "Young Voices," a poem that both remembers a time of youth and praises the young.

Which is, of course, not to say he didn't get tired of students and words, tired of maneuvering and cloaking exhaustion with duty. Sure he did, and said that and more in "Ennui," a poem about the clutter of a busy life, one filled with love and work, delight and boredom. So many of us feel the same way, but Tomás gave tongue to our feelings.

It is late winter in 1983, probably as warm in Riverside, California, from where Chancellor Rivera is calling me, as it is in San Antonio. So the weather has nothing to do with this:

7

"Frank, it's me, Tomás. I'm thinking about going back into teaching. My wife's right. I'm only happy when I'm writing and teaching. What do you know about that might be good for me to look into?"

"We're going to start interviewing for a distinguished chair. Why don't you consider that?"

"Do you really think I'm qualified?"

"If you're not, who is?"

He came to see us in the early spring with the same *brío*, the same common man. But his hair was greying, and his grip was not as strong. Later he called and said that he had too many projects underway as chancellor and had withdrawn his name. The next time I heard about him, he was dead. We could write all the lies of life by beginning each sentence with *if* and *perhaps*.

Tomás knew this, and entwined life and death in all he wrote. Aware of what might be, he lived what he had. And he would meet you on your own level, any level you had or wanted, as I recall in reading again "Run, Puff, Run, Run." This is a serious poem, no laughter here. But I laughed as I read the puffing, see Tomás moving fast down the street.

"Frank, I just got back from a meeting in Madrid. How're you doing?"

"Good. How was Madrid?"

"Man, they almost killed me."

"Almost killed you! Who almost killed you?"

"Some shoeshine guys. I took a walk after lunch while everyone else was taking a nap. This guy came up to me and said he wanted to shine my shoes. I told him no. No one but me shines my shoes. But he wouldn't stop asking me. Then he grabbed my arm and shouted: 'Let me shine your shoes!' I clipped him on the jaw, laid him out on the sidewalk, and kept on walking. He got up and started banging two shoebrushes together. Frank, shoeshine guys came from everywhere. There must have been 25 or 30. I ran like hell and got back to where I was staying before they could catch me. But it was too close."

I tell Tomás I only lost $12.50 on a glass of applejuice for a lovely flamenco dancer when I was in Madrid. He was not amused.

Felipe Reyes and I are in my dining room, cutting and pasting Tomás' poems and Felipe's drawings onto pages. Felipe has already drawn the

8

cover as Tomás wanted it: a brick wall with words painted on it—just like in the barrio: *Always and Other Poems*. We stop over one poem, talk about it and question its truth:

> What if I were to remain
> here
> in the words
> forever?

But now the words seem all we have left of our friend, Tomás Rivera. His family has more, we say to ourselves; and that pleases us. Yet we may have more than the words, too. In any case, the words will do.

Frank Kersnowski
Trinity University
San Antonio, Texas

9

Introduction

Searching is a constant theme in the work of Tomás Rivera. We find it in his landmark novel, *... y no se lo tragó la tierra/ ... and the earth did not devour him*,[1] where the Chicano migrant workers are constantly searching for work and, spiritually, searching for a sense of community, and where the young protagonist searches for his past and his identity. We find the same theme in his collection of short fiction, *The Harvest/La cosecha*[2] and also in his poetry, most notably and appropriately, in the epic *The Searchers*.

The theme of searching can be applied to various levels: the search for material gain and economic improvment; the quest for community and a rightful place in society; the search for self-determination and a voice in this country's political establishment; and also the pursuit of meaning which concerns all intellectual endeavors. The figure of the migrant worker is a complex metaphor for all these levels of searching.

In his article, "Into the Labyrinth: The Chicano in Literature," Rivera uses the labyrinth as a form of literature through which one searches for meaning:

> Literature, and fiction, provide tension. Literature represents man's life, it also reflects his inner search and his outward search. It is, in a sense, an intricate maze to provide either exteriorization or internalization of the human involvement and evolvement ... And the search can only exist if there is an impulse into the labyrinth of the human totality of conditions. Thus, the search and labyrinth complement each other to bring forth a vicarious sensibility to the perceiver.[3]

For Rivera, the labyrinth is also the means by which one searches for one's alter ego, the 'other': "It is a vicarious notion of humanity, or man, to attempt to search for the other 'alter ego' in order to better comprehend himself ... the labyrinth ... is a mold wherein he can place his life. In essence, is it not life in search of form—a conquest, a labyrinth in which to reflect his human condition?" (*Labyrinth* 18). Rivera discovers his 'other' in Chicano literature: "for me the literary experience is one of total communion, an awesome awareness of the 'other,' of one's potential self. I have come to recognize my 'other' in Chicano literature."[4] For Rivera, the literary experience—reading and writing—is "a personal ritual" whereby one establishes "contact with humanity and with one's origins" (*Fiesta* 452). This is the experience that the young protagonist of *Tierra* undergoes when he "finds" his people, *la raza*, and merges with their collective memory and experience.

Implied in Rivera's discussion of the literary process is that the search itself is a figure, in a tropological sense. As we read *Tierra*, for example, its fragmented structure resembles a labyrinth, the successful passage through which entails that we comprehend the search as a figure of writing, as an allegory of the creative process. This fragmented structure is itself a duplication of the mind of the young protagonist who strives to give external form—literature—to the chaos of his experience and unresolved identity. The search, then, involves two complementary goals. One is ontological, the search for meaning and the 'other,' and the other is aesthetic: the search is "An exact, pure desire to transform what is isolated in the mind into an external form" (*Fiesta* 439).

In the search for the form in which to mold the Chicano experience, the Chicano needs to invent his own labyrinth, as Rivera affirms:

> This brings us to the Chicano ... who also wishes to create a labyrinth, who wishes to invent himself in the labyrinth ... where he can vicariously live his total human condition. However, since he has perceived continually the development of the North American and the Mexican literatures, literatures which have reached great heights of intricateness and sophistication for their counterparts, more stress is given to finding form or forms for expression. So we find Chicano literature and the Chicanos in fiction as simply life in search of form. (*Labyrinth* 19)

In the poetry which you, the reader, are about to experience, you will encounter the theme of searching in its various manifestations and levels.

Tomás Rivera was born to a family of migrant farmworkers in the south Texas town of Crystal City, on December 22, 1935. From his early years until 1954, Rivera traveled with his family, joining the migrant stream that left the winter garden area of Crystal City around mid-April, searching for farmwork as far north as Michigan and Minnesota, and returning around the beginning of November. This nomadic life required that Rivera make up much school work upon his return to Crystal City, which became impossible when he began junior college in 1954. He then could only join his family during the summer months.[5] Rivera would later document the experiences of the migrant farmworker in his monumental novel, ... *y no se lo tragó la tierra*.

Upon completion of junior college, he attended Southwest Texas State Teachers College, in San Marcos, receiving a B.S. in English Education in 1958. He taught English and Spanish in various high schools, until he returned to Southwest Texas to complete his M.Ed., in 1964. In 1966 he commenced graduate studies in Spanish literature at the University of Oklahoma, receiving his Ph.D. in 1969. After teaching two years at Sam Houston State University, he took a position at The University of Texas at San Antonio, where he shortly became Vice President for Administration in 1976. From 1978–79, he was Executive Vice President of the University of Texas at El Paso. The following year he received the appointment of Chancellor of the University of California at Riverside, a position he held until his sudden death in May, 1984. With his death, Tomás Rivera had published twenty-six poems and had left a slightly larger amount unpublished. The first part of this collection contains those published poems, while the second part presents an equal number of the unpublished poems.[6] In his "Poetics," Rivera states that "poetry should not be explained, categorized, studied, but read and felt and sung." Poetry was for Rivera a very intimate experience. And from his words, I also gather—and this is the sense I get from reading his poetry—that poetry, by and large, was for him a private experience. His fiction he wrote for his people; his poetry he wrote for himself. The exception in this regard is "The Searchers," an epic which, by definition, is public poetry. Most of his poetry, however, is intensely lyrical; Rivera writes it for and to himself. Like many of those Renaissance writers who died keeping their lyric poetry to themselves, only to have editors ferret it out and publish it after their death, so too Rivera left much of his poetry— certainly unintentionally—for this editor to publish posthumously. However, in keeping with Rivera's words and as part of my editorial bargain, I shall attempt to restrain my explications and to keep this introduction brief.

The theme of the migrant worker, which permeates Rivera's prose, is found, implicity and explicitly, in only four of these poems: in "The Rooster Crows en Iowa y en Texas"—where the rooster's crows symbolize an unending cycle of work and schooling both in the north and at home in Texas, in "The Overalls"— which introduces the speaker to the enigma of death, in "Noon-Night"—which is notable for its accusatory tone and the shackles of evil, and in "The Searchers," where the migrant workers and their quest are this epic's subject and theme.

"The Searchers" can be considered the *summa* of Rivera's poetic achievement. Incorporating the major themes and motifs of his lyric poetry, this epic is a notable achievement in the American grain. Rivera saw in his people, the migrant workers, that same spiritual nobility and search that brought all immigrants to this country, indeed, to all the Americas:

13

I think of the whole American scene—both continents—and the fact that we have transplanted cultures from Europe, and the fact of the indigenous cultures still being here. I wanted to document that, but I also wanted to throw light on the spiritual strength, on the concept of justice so important for the American continents. I wanted to treat the idea of mental and intellectual liberation and where it fits into the spectrum of the Americas. Can it be achieved here, and if so, can it be done? ... creo que aquí tenemos la capacidad y la posibilidad de una emancipación intelectual mucho más fuerte y total [I think that here we have the capacity and possibility of a much stronger and complete intellectual emancipation]. Within those migrants I saw that strength. They may be economically deprived, politically deprived, socially deprived, but they kept moving, never staying in one place to suffer or be subdued, sino siempre buscaban trabajo [but always searching for work]. Siempre andaban buscando [they always kept searching]; that's why they were "migrant" workers. La palabra *trabajador* está muy implícita allí [The word *worker* is very implicit there]; they were travelers. If they stayed where there was no work se morían [they would die], y no se murieron [and they didn't die]. I see that same sense of movement in the Europeans who came here, and that concept of justicia espiritual también [spiritual justice, too]. It was there. And the migrant workers still have that role: to be searchers. I've written a poem called "The Searchers." Para mí era gente que buscaba [To me they were people who searched], and that's an important metaphor in the Americas. My grandfather was a searcher; my father was a searcher; I hope I can also be a searcher. That's the spirit I seek. (*Inquiry* 73).

"The Searchers" has three principal intentions.[7] The first is the affirmation of a spiritual nobility which is manifested in the persistent search for justice and the realization of the Chicano's potential existence. In this regard, the epic, true to its tradition, recounts an odyssey and expresses the collective sentiment of the Chicanos, *la raza*:

> How long
> how long
> have we been searchers?
> We have been
> behind the door
> Always behind screens and eyes
> of other eyes
> We longed to search

14

Always
longed to search (...)
We searched through
our own voices
and through
our own minds
We sought with our words

Here we note an allusion to the labyrinth in which the quest for being and identity parallels the search and discovery of form, which constitutes the epic's second intention. While the poem's narrative level sets forth the search for full existence, the Chicano's rightful place in society, the allegorical level expresses the search for form:

From within came
the passions to create
of every clod and stone
a new life
a new dream
each day
In these very things
we searched
as we crumbled
dust, our very own
imaginary beings (...)
A terrón lighted our eyes
and we watered it and made
mud-clay
to create others in

While the lines in English allegorically express the search for form, the poem embeds lines in Spanish that achieved their form centuries ago and which are readily recognizable as *poesía popular*: "naranja dulce / limón partido / dame un abrazo / que yo te pido."[8] The Spanish verse forms derive from the folklore tradition, which is a major component in Rivera's work, and which is reflected in his use of *corridos* and allusions to and employment of other oral literary forms.[9] Hence, we note in "The Searchers" the integration of this oral form within a written epic—itself originally an oral literature—in search of a more comprehensive form, and one that will express the bicultural and bilingual components of the Chicano artist.

The search and discovery of literary form makes possible the epic's third intention: the search into the past in order to rescue the dead, and, through this resurrection, achieve the salvation of the living:

> Death
> We searched in Death
> We contemplated the original
> and searched
> and savored it
> only to find profound
> beckoning
> A source that continued the search
> beyond creation and death
> The mystery
> The mystery of our eyes
> The eyes we have as
> spiritual reflection
> and we found we were
> not alone

In the search through the zone of death, through the creative space of solitude, the living and the dead are united. Similar to the experience of the young protagonist in *Tierra*, as Rivera affirms, "It is from the past that we are able to perceive, create and give life [to] our ritual; it is from this that we derive strength, that we can recognize our existence as human beings" (*Fiesta* 440). Through memory the Chicanos encounter their salvation, discovering that "We are not alone," and that they carry within themselves the history and collective experience of their people.

The reunification of the dead and the living is formally achieved through parallelism, a common oral device:

> We are not alone ...
> when Chona ...
> a mythic Chicana,
> died in the sugar beet fields ...
> or when that truck filled with us
> went off the mountain road (...)
> We were not alone in Iowa
> when we slept in wet ditches
> frightened by salamanders (...)
> We were not alone
> when we created children (...)
> We are not alone
> after many centuries

16

Through the modulation of the refrain—"We are not alone/We were not alone"—and its juxtapostion with the past and present, time is eternalized and the dead and the living exist contemporaneously. In their memory and collective conscious, the Chicanos live together. Memory and literary form, thus, make possible the rescue of the dead, the recuperation of the spirit of the search, the salvation of the living and the realization of continuity. "Chicano writing," declares Rivera, "is a ritual of immortality ... a ritual of the living ... a fiesta of the living" (*Fiesta* 439). By virtue of literary creation, the Chicano gains his existence and thereby becomes aware of the continuity of Chicano culture: "We have been alive since time began" (*Fiesta* 440).

Death, in its various masks, is a constant theme in Rivera's work. One of its masks is that death caused by hardship and injustice, as doña Chona's in "The Searchers" or the children's in some stories of *Tierra*. Another death is the eventual loss of a loved one, such as the father whose empty overalls are "in the garage, hanging." Another of death's masks is what Rivera calls "original death." This appears to have, for Rivera, two different but experentially similar manifestations. On the one hand, it is an archetypal death, such as that related in "The Searchers" or, most hauntingly, in the short story "The Salamanders."[10] On the other, "original death" is that experience derived from the aesthetic moment, as Rivera implies in his "Poetics": "Poetry gives me pure feelings—time, beauty, man and original death." Whether it be encountered, such as in "The Salamanders," or deliberately sought through memory and the creative acts, "original death" is paradoxically the dissolution of the self and its plenitude, a nirvana-like state that tastes of eternity. Through "original death" one is reborn, and Rivera seeks it out in quest of an infinite series of rebirths.

Although a search by definition points to a goal or something as the object of that search, for Rivera the search is also its own objective, as he states in "Poetics"—"Poetry is finding the search"—, and again expresses in "Searching at Leal Middle School" and insinuates in other poems. Thus, while the search leads to discovery, it is the search itself, the act of discovering, the creative act, that Rivera seeks.

In the second section of *The Searchers: Collected Poetry*, among those poems that Rivera left unpublished, the theme and act of searching is repeatedly expressed. Here we encounter the search for the other and the dead—"Las voces del olvido"/"Do Not Forget Me," "Another Day," "Eternity"—, the search for the past, not only in order to rescue it but also to be free of it—"La vida por fin empezó"/"Finally Life Began," "Desátate—, and, consistently emphasized, the search for the creative act: "Searching at Leal Middle School," "Nacimiento"/"Birth," "El des-

17

pertar"/"Awakening," "Palabras," "Soy una palabra."

An important symbol of the search and the act of discovering is the dump. It first appears in *Tierra*, in the story "It's That It Hurts," and reappears in "Searching at Leal Middle School." In an interview, Rivera explains the importance of the dump: "My dad knew I liked to read, so ... We ... used to go to the dump to collect reading materials. I found encyclopedias and different types of books. At home I still have my dump collection gathered from the dumps in northern towns. People threw away a lot of books" (*Inquiry* 143).

The dump is the subject of a poem that appears to be incomplete. Existing only in an autograph state and without a title, and not wanting to just relegate it to an archival box, I reproduce and transcribe this intensely lyrical piece.

[In the Dump]

In the dump
he discovered beautiful flowers
among the cans and broken bottles
and tires worn out.
The sky was blue blue
and even the birds looked at it
and didn't disturb its beauty
with their flight
a sacred blue, pushing toward the earth
encircling his cosmos
pushing his
eyes inward until he would
fall asleep.
He also saw ants
winding slowly toward him
and past him in solitary communion
gasping life through tin can cities
and glass cages among rusty lakes
and giant trees moving their search
among each other when the wind dared.
He wanted to search
to wind slowly with them
and to fly high until he would
touch it.
He reached out and found no search
only the sky and its blue
suffocating his eyes
until he only heard a white line.

18

In the dump

he discovered beautiful flowers
among the cans and broken bottles
and was ties worn out.
The sky was blue blue
and even the birds looked at it
and didn't disturb its beauty
with their flight
A sea blue, pushing toward the earth
invading his cosmos spreading his
eyes inward until he would
fall asleep.

He also saw ants
winding slowly toward him
and past him in solitary communion
gasping off life through tin can cities
and glass cages among misty lakes
and giant trees reading searching
                    moving their search
among each other when the wind died.

He wanted to search
and wind slowly with them
and to fly high until he would
touch. #
He reached out and found no search
but only the sky and its blue
suffocating filling his eyes, suffocating them
until he saw only heard only a white line.

The poem presents a few textual problems; for example, the phrase "when the wind dared" is vague due to the lack of a predicate compliment, that is, what the wind dares to do is not expressed nor is it implied. Nor is it clear what the direct object pronoun, possibly deleted, of "touch it" refers to: is it the "search" of the next line or the sky of line five and of the antepenultimate line?

The poem's textual and semantic incompleteness, and the synesthetic oxymora of the last two lines contribute to the poem's enigmatic quality. However, drawing from those texts in which the dump appears, the poem's subject is presumably an adolescent who discovers in the dump, that which has been thrown away as refuse, objects of beauty. In the dump the subject endeavors to find the search but it appears to elude him. Yet the final line suggests a liminal state, the entrance into that creative solitude that augurs the process of discovery and rebirth. It is clear that the dump, that mountain of refuse into which *la raza* had and has been thrown, is a symbol of search, of discovery and self-discovery which Rivera kept writing about in his fiction, essays and in this poetry he has left us.

I wish to express my gratitude to the National Endowment for the Humanities and to the University of Houston for the travel grants that allowed me do research at the Tomás Rivera Archives, University of California, Riverside, and which made possible this complete collection of the poetry of Tomás Rivera. I also acknowledge the assistance of Mr. Armand Martínez-Standifird, archivist of the Rivera papers, and I especially thank Mrs. Concepción Rivera for her enthusiastic support.

Julián Olivares
University of Houston
17.III.90

The Searchers: Collected Poetry

I

Poetics

Poetry is one of the most human of experiences because it begins with nothing. It is the birth and death of the word and the poet, as he freezes abstractions, severs relationships with his utterances. Poetry is finding the search, finding the word. It is not inventing, but finding, starting the invention. Yet poetry should not be explained, categorized, studied, but read and felt and sung. Poetry denies the poet but not his expression and utterance. Poetry, then, is a way of becoming nothing and everything. In a way, poetry is and is not what Octavio Paz says: "knowledge, salvation, power, abandonment." Poetry gives me pure feelings—time, beauty, man and original death.

The Rooster Crows en Iowa y en Texas

The rooster crows.
The alarm rings.
They eat and go to work.

"Aladín y su lámpara maravillosa"

The snow falls.
The truck runs full of people.
And we return . . . . home.

"Once upon a time there were three little pigs"

To spend money.
And to walk in the holes
full of street
of my town.

The street calls and
extends itself
to the house of the door
and the fence of the gate
and . . .

I look . . .
It looks at me . . .
yawns and shakes its dust.

And I yawn and sleep
until the rooster crows.

De niño   De joven   De viejo

El vidrio que brilla
en el césped, azul,
la boca que habla
con sonora sonrisa.

El sol que calienta
las sienes repletas
de ganas de risas
de juegos de grandes.

La mañana refresca
los sueños soñados.
Las ventanas que se abren
a paredes de vida.

Las puertas abiertas.
Los pasos contentos.
Los tientos de carne
que dan calor.

Los cuentos contados
son los sueños soñados
de pasos contentos
de sienes repletas.

Cada mañana
la frescura
le limpia la cara,
le abre los ojos,
le da una sonrisa,
le mueve los pies.

Y el ñino
se mueve en un mundo
y empieza a soñar

* * *

La casa que huele
a sol apagado
que a veces alumbra
sin saber por qué.

La puerta cerrada
que no quiere abrirse.
Los pasos cauteles,
las sonrisas fingidas,
los pesares pesando
la noche sin fin.

La ventana cerrada.
La mañana caliente
que hace sudar.
El día sin fin
con odios y amores
y sordos temores.

Las miradas abajo,
pensadas sentencias.
Los dientes cerrados
detrás labios hambrientos
en noches de días
tan largos.

La vida sin rumbo
como sueños de sed,
las vidas y vida

sin saber por qué.

Cada mañana
el calor
le suda la cara,
le cierra los ojos,
para despertarlo
a un nuevo soñar.

* * *

Los sueños pasados,
los viejos amigos,
las tardes sueñosas,
las manos cerradas.

Las mañanas oscuras,
sin seña de vida.
La puerta entreabierta
a otro nuevo soñar.

El sol penetrante
por cabellos resecos
sin vida y color.
Un ruido secreto
de otro vivir.

La boca, los ojos,
los dientes que tragan,
la lengua hecha nudo.
Garganta reseca
de palabras ya muertas
por tanto vividas.

La ventana entreabierta

al recuerdo pasado
de paredes de vida
y vidrio que brilla.

La noche sin fin,
la boca que habla
con sonora risa
de labios hambrientos.

La vida,
la vida, sin rumbo,
le limpia la cara,
le cierra los ojos,
le dice un secreto,
uno de tantos
secretos ruidosos.

De niño, de joven, de viejo,
todo,
todo fue un soñar.

Hide the Old People
or
American Idearium

"A la víbora, víbora de la mar,
de la mar,
por aquí pueden pasar.
Los de adelante corren mucho y
los de atrás se quedarán."

Escóndanlos.
Escóndanlos bien.
Escóndanlos en la casona grande y lujosa,
Escóndanlos.

¡Que nadie los vea, ya están muy viejos!
¡Son puro trabajo,
no valen la pena ya!
¡Que no nos miren!
si ya no nos conocen.

Ellos ya se gastaron.

Escóndanlos.

"Los de adelante corren mucho y
los de atrás se quedarán."

Siempre el domingo

Vayan a la iglesia el domingo
y rueguen por yo pecador,
mientras

yo veo la ametralladora japonesa
y las paracaídas alemanas
y las banderas italianas
y los retratos de tantos hombres muertos
en *Veteran's Place*.

¡Que me hallen allí en la cantina!
¡Que miren las bayonetas
y las banderas
y a Villa
y a Pershing
y a Obregón
y a Ike
y a Carranza
y a mi cuate
y a todos esos hombres muertos
en las guerras!

¡Que nos miren bailar!
¡Que miren que vivimos
como ellos lo quisieran!

Vayan a la iglesia y recen por su salvación.
Yo me voy
a la cantina
a bailarles y
a divertirles
a tantos hombres muertos

mientras
las botellas regurgitan.

Odio

Weeds rupture the marble
and I laugh at the whiteness.
Alone,
daggers,
knifing,
soundless,
unloved through death.
Torn from the earth,
left to dry,
to die.

Future in the seed.

Stone upon stone
of despair.
Stone from which
come the weeds
who blade each other
without love
        to be torn from the earth
        and thrown to the earth.

The seed is here
on the stone
on my forehead.

M'ijo no mira nada

—Mira, m'ijo, qué rascacielo.
"Does it reach the sky and heaven?"
—Mira, m'ijo, qué carrazo.
"Can it get to the end of the world?"
—Mira, m'ijo, ese soldado.
"¿Por qué pelea?"
—Mira, m'ijo, qué bonita fuente.
"Yes, but I want to go to the restrooom."
—Mira, m'ijo, qué tiendota de J. C. Penney,
allí trabajarás un día.
"Do you know the people there, daddy?"
—No,
vámonos a casa,
tú no miras nada.

Me lo enterraron

Yo no, ellos,
ellos me lo enterraron.
Ellos no sabían
que traía su anillote con su M bien grabada,
que siempre nos traía pan dulce por las noches,
que nunca iba a la iglesia pero sabía amar,
que amaba mucho a mi madre pero tenía su "vieja."

Ellos no sabían
que me enseñó a llorar y a amar,
que me pateaba por un quinto y después lloraba,
que siempre trabajaba,
y que cantaba, y que amaba.

Ellos no lo sabían.
Y por eso me lo enterraron.
Yo no quería.
Yo no lo enterré.

Seeds in the Hour of Seeds

Dawn light
fractured by profiles
Touches of life breathing

Anticipated death
prevails
in exhaling essence
Dawn light
separating your profile

The seed,
mine,
yours,
is here, alive
We
One

Have we liberated light?

Full . . . now
Profiles . . .
You triumph
as light
totally prevails

You,
our son, and me
isolated by light

You,
our son,
seeds we are

in prime light
in dawn light
in the hour of seeds

Young Voices

Young voices,
fresh, loved by the wind
Grasped
delighted
held by the wind

New voices
young voices
who soften the wind
eternally loved
carved forever
into the wind

In the night
the wind is a lover
of young voices
of love seeds
scattered
pollen
eternal

For the voice
is the love seed
in the dark

Perfection of Perfections

Hands entwined
through arms and waists

perfection of perfections
the young bodies

Beauty,
no more beauty than this
there is

in the night
in the night
in the night

to never wait for the light
to savor love
the crystallization of their beauty

Do they know?

Yes

Always

You have seen yourself
for you have been looking
out the door

Always

You never sleep
        never dream
You wait for yourself

Always

You have seen yourself
You were here before
many
yesterday
today
ever
behind the door

Always

Another Me

There must be
there has to be
another me

For how would I know,
why would I want to know?

There must be
there has to be
another me

Our children
am I in them or
they in me?

I was the leaf
that I know

This Solitude

solitude, dark, blackness
through powers of the body
grasping of me
puzzlement
through eyes
unwanting

grasping tightly
images of despair
bits of light, rays
contemplation of sorrows

dull upon dullness
sitting on every dream
so distant now
so distant
so damning to this life
to this darkness
to this solitude
to this dark
     waning
        nodding
           smile

The Overalls

Frightening
as the attic hole
the overalls in the garage, hanging
and the vapor from the train
swung to my face
as the cross that
shouted the lump
in the cemetery
and the sounds of clods
of earth hitting the coffin
reminded me of something
I knew nothing about
the glancing of tearful eyes
embracing
as I sensed
that I had been born
the crushing vapor
and the overalls, hanging
in the garage
never to be filled again

Soundless words

Words without sound
how terribly deaf

What if I were to remain
here
in the words
forever?

A Most Tired Word

Love
a most tired word
replacement needed
overused
abused
love
a most tired word
beyond hollowness
seeking itself
it is

Past Possessions

A piece of string
A broken top
A crooked kite
A wooden gun
A mop ...

Quiet ... noise

A long thin weed a lance
A few large cans a dance
   Boxes
For car and houses

Such trivial things

Run, Puff, Run, Run

We look and see
We come and go

An arm, legs, a head
to be filled
to be filled

Not to think
Not to love
Not to move

To be filled
To be filled

not to be

Jump, jump

Run, puff, run, run

Ennui

desk	pencil	voices
people	words	faces
cars	windows	clothes
paper	war	children
towns	houses	cities
nations	presidents	laws
joy	death	sorrow
religion		
man		
stars		
dirt		
flowers		
animals		
birth		
world		
worlds		

Autumn and Winter

The wind
The beauty
The cold air

humbles the people

The sun
The leaves
The broken twigs

they bow their humility

Reminders

to bend the head
in chest, and
to suck in a
death-smelling air
while the wind and cold
circle the sun

One last gaze at the warm beauty

When Love To Be

When love to be?
when
leaves warmly cover
protectingly from
sun and snow and wind
and feet
everyone will walk toward me
not away
when
love to be
comes
now, no one listens

I've been ready for so long

since many times
of leaves covering
warmly to protect
yet dying
from sun and snow and wind
and feet

I've been ready for so long

when love to be
will everyone walk toward me
and stay?

The Child

The child spoke
as the man spoke
as the child spoke
to understand
each other's
death.

The Eyes of a Child

First, the color,
then the comprehension
of a limitless love.

The eyes of a child
must surely touch.
Its color

Unknown comprehension
open to be shut
open to create.

Color, form, limitless eyes
of a limitless love.

The eyes of a child can touch
The eyes of a child can feel
The eyes of a child can be.

Do they know that we know?

Alone

I am alone
because of the street
and the faces.

I almost spoke to one
once.
Starting is difficult.

I am alone
and the street is long
and the faces

Can't stop.

Shouldn't follow it.

Now, I am really alone
Can't stop.

Perhaps
if I walk backwards with the faces.

A Blas de Otero

La cicatriz del pecado original:
Anonadada la justicia y
el pecado original sobre
las tumbas
encuentran el delirio
de una acción asesinada.

Vuelve a ver al niño
mírale la frente
que allí está el diente
del odio
hundido.

Y por los ojos
sedientos y proféticos
y los brazos añorando
de la madre
que estira la mano
en sueños de pesetas
cayendo por los cielos

sin pan,
sin pan haber nacido
la cicatriz del pecado original
con hambre y sed.

The Searchers

I

How long
how long
have we been searchers?

We have been
behind the door
Always
behind screens and eyes
of other eyes
We longed to search
Always
longed to search

naranja dulce
limón partido
dame un abrazo
que yo te pido

We searched through
our own voices
and through
our own minds
We sought with our words

A la víbora, víbora
de la mar
de la mar
por aquí pueden pasar

How those words

lighted our eyes
From within came
the passions to create
of every clod and stone
a new life
a new dream
each day
In these very things
we searched
as we crumbled
dust, our very own
imaginary beings

Hey, ese vato, chíngate

A terrón lighted our eyes
and we watered it and made
mud-clay
to create others in

II

The search begun
so many years ago only
to feel the loneliness
of centuries
Hollow—soundless centuries
without earth

How can we be alone
How can we be alone
if we are so close to the earth?

Tierra eres
Tierra serás
Tierra te volverás

Una noche caminando
una sombra negra vi
Yo me separaba de ella
y ella se acercaba a mí.

¿Qué anda haciendo, caballero?
¿Qué anda haciendo por aquí?
Ando en busca de mi esposa
que se separó de mí.

Su esposa ya no está aquí
su esposa ya se murió
Cuatro candeleros blancos
son los que alumbran allí.

III

Death
We searched in Death
We contemplated the original
and searched
and savored it
only to find profound
beckoning
A source that continued the search
beyond creation and death
The mystery
The mystery of our eyes
The eyes we have as
spiritual reflection
and we found we were
not alone

In our solitude
we found our very being
We moved into each other's

almost carefully, deliberately

Had we been here before?
What do we have, you and I?
Only our touch, our feeling
shared, that is all that we have
life in such ways, way
again, again, again
We found ourselves in ourselves
and while touching
we found other mysteries
that lay beneath
every layer of truth
unwinding each finding
another lonely vigil
another want, desire
to find
to find what?
What we always had?
Did anyone know that we
were searching?
That every look toward the earth
was a penetrating search that
had lasted for years
the mystery of time halted
and unkown without
itself discovery

IV

At night we searched each other
Somewhere was the soul
Somewhere in there was the heart
Somewhere in the night
was the lonely eye of the soul
Motionless

Waiting

Sometimes we found it
and slept with our lips
on it till the light fractured
everything

Can we find something every day
and every night?
We believed
yes, we had been finding
for centuries

Other beings?
We,
one,
the very same flavor
the very same
We looked behind heads
at the back of heads
The back of white heads
was less dangerous
Sometimes we turned the
heads around only to find
eyes that didn't see
who dared not see
who dared not be
within our own

No estamos solos.

V

We are not alone
if we remember and
recollect our passions

through the years
the giving of hands and backs
"dale los hombros a tus hijos"
We are not alone
Our eyes still meet with the passion
of continuity and prophecy

We are not alone
when we were whipped
in school for losing
the place in the book
or for speaking Spanish
on the school grounds
or
when Chona,
dear Chona,
a mythic Chicana,
died in the sugar beet fields
with her eight-month
child
buried deep within her
still
or
when that truck
filled with us
went off the mountain road
in Utah
with screams
eternally etched among
the mountain snows

We were not alone in death

VI

We were not alone in Iowa

When we slept in wet ditches
frightened by salamanders
at night
reclaiming their territory
and we
killing them
to maintain it as our—
then, our only—posssession
or
in San Angelo
when we visited the desiccated
tubercular bodies of
aunts and uncles
friends and lovers

We were not alone
when we created children
and looked into their eyes
and searched for perfection
We were not alone
when taught
the magic of a smile, a kiss
an embrace each morning
and to feel the warmth
and quiver of a human
being

We were not alone
murmuring the novenas,
los rosarios, each night,
los rosarios we hoped
would bring joy and lasting peace
for Kiko
killed and buried in Italy in 1943
or

when we gathered each night
before bed
and waited
for the nightly sound
of the familiar cough
and the sweet/pan dulce
that it brought
Warm milk/pan dulce
opened the evening door
or
when we walked
all over Minnesota
looking for work
No one seemed to care
we did not expect them to care

VII

We were not alone
after many centuries
How could we be alone
We searched together
We were seekers
We are searchers
and we will continue
to search
because our eyes
still have
the passion of prophecy.

II

Searching at Leal Middle School

December 11,
Thursday,
foggy day,
morning,
a good day for searching.
I discovered children through the fog
bundles, bultos,
manos en la bolsa turning
bultos in serenity
Leal
Apellido hispano
Who was Leal?
What had he/she done to deserve
his/her name as household word
known by hundreds of students
year after year.

"Yo voy a la Leal"

At first I saw only
the backs of black hair heads
Cabezas de pelo negro, negro era
Cabezas de pelo negro
brillante, de brillo, brillo era
and as
I went to the front of the room
to face them
I saw their limitless eyes
ojos sin límites
ojos oscuros
ojos sonrientes,
juguetones

— ¿Y éste?

We talked of thinking
    of inventing ourselves
    of love for others
    of love to be
    of searching
for ourselves

It was a good day for searching
Yet I became lost in my past
I saw myself and became
each one for an instant
and grasped for a second
the curious blink.
In split instances I became
the student, silent, staring
beyond myself, backwards
to joys so long forgotten of long
roads,
dusty roads
that went forever,
and friends
running toward me
from far away.
Away in the dump yards
where smoke curled and
with long sticks we turned and turned and
found half-rotten fruit
to be washed and eaten
and books—
Livingston's exploration of Africa,
the maps,
the blacks,
I became Henry L. in the forest—

and other books
of diseases and red, blue,
brown and purple organs
and more books discarded by
the rich
(the strange word)
and magazines
I searched for words in the dump
I saw doña Cuquita again:

"Cuidado con la lumbre.
Donde hay humito, hay lumbre por debajo."

And her apron
long apron rolled up
heavy with sweet-smoked fruit
sitting down to eat and listen
cobwebbed eye lashes could not
hide her dark eyes
ojos oscuros que fascinan
Did she know about Livingston?
Through the smoke.

I saw bultos
I discovered bundles of
manos en la bolsa,
children
Monday 11,
Thursday,
foggy day,
a good day for finding at
Leal Middle School.
And now, in the future,
I will search for it also
and for a few

cabezas de pelo negro
de ojos oscuros.

En la hora de las semillas

Albor ...
 fracturado por los perfiles.
Tientos
de vida ... respiración.
La muerte prevalece,
anticipada exacta
en la aspiración.

Albor
que separa los perfiles.

La semilla,
tuya,
mía,
está aquí, viva,
entre nosotros.

¿Hemos liberado luz?

Llenos ahora,
los perfiles
triunfan, se construyen
al imponerse la luz.

Tú,
nuestro hijo,
volvemos a las primas semillas.

En la luz prima,
en el albor,
en la hora de las semillas.

Noon-Night

To hate him, anyone,
a white face, why
everyone.
You see this sore, on my knee
and on his
and on hers
on all of us?
We will never be cured.
But I guarantee
you will not do it to my son
nor to my daughter.
They will not kneel, not bend.
I'll remind them,
I'll tell them of the old times
when dust choked this throat
and when I was hit and laughed at,
when I was made to eat shit
in a taco—laughing, all laughing.
To hate him, anyone.
I'm silent. I am quiet.
I am not free.
I'm discovering evil.

noon-night

To hate him, anyone
a white face, why
everyone.
You see this sore, on my knee
and on his
and on hers
on all of us
we will never be cured
but I guarantee
you will not do it to my son
nor to my daughter
they will not kneel, not bend.

I'll remind them,
I'll tell them of the old times
when dust choked this throat
and when I was hit and laughed at
when I was made to eat shit
in a taco — laughing, all laughing
to hate him, anyone...
I'm silent. I keep quiet quiet
I'm drawing evil with you,

Las voces del olvido

Las voces del olvido
me hablaron del presente
y me dijeron
"no me olvides."

Recuerdos
de siglos durmientes
de tantos despertar
de anochecer
de amanecer.

Las voces del olvido
me despiertan al futuro
Recuerdos
de siglos venideros
de tantos despertar
de amanecer
de anochecer.

Y oigo que me dice
mi otro
"no me olvides."

Do Not Forget Me

When I am silent
I always hear dark voices
far away
in me.
They always say,
"Do not forget me."

I must have known them
centuries
ago,
sleeping.
At times, then,
when some being of mine
was awakened,
I also felt the desire to leave
through that pulsating tunnel.

One day,
I was awakened
and I walked out
into the brillance.

It was then that
I heard for the first time,
all my beings,
"Do not forget me."

Nacimiento

Los colores nacen
a cada instante.

¿Entra o se despega de la luz?

El instante forma las líneas,
forma los colores
y abre luz
y abre luz.

Los colores nacen,
engrandecimiento,
amplificación exacta
en cada forma.

Verificar, verificar.

Los colores nacen
para crear.

El despertar

Cuando todo es nada
y nada está en todo
me ciego en el instante.

Nada está en todo.

Los sentidos me matan.

Muero,
muero al despertar
en el mundo.

Y espero
Y espero

Cuando nada esté en todo
para siempre
y lo perfectamente blanco
me circunde.

Awakening

When everything is nothing
and nothing is in everything
I blind myself in the instant.

Nothing is in everything.

My senses execute me.

I die
I die upon awakening
in the world.

And I wait
and I must wait
until nothing will be in everything

forever
and the perfectly white surrounds me.

Palabras

En esta hoja blanca
dejo caer pedazos vivos de sesos
Aquí me quedo para siempre
Ahora ya me conocen
Detrás de cada letra mis ojos les siguen
Los veo, yo los veo, a ustedes
No quiero salir de aquí
Aquí estoy para siempre
Qué fácil fue romper
el secreto eterno.
¿Por qué no me siguen?
Métanse conmigo entre las palabras.
Juguemos entre ellas, dejemos que
caigan sobre nuestro cuerpo
Amontonémoslas sobre nuestro ombligo
Echémoslas al aire
Leámoslas, amémoslas
que están sedientas de amor
Engendrémoslas, repletémoslas
hasta que salgan de nuestra boca
con ganas.
Por eso en esta hoja blanca
he dejado caer pedazos de sesos
manchados de sangre que
huelen a vida y que sabrán vivir.
Y el secreto ¿qué fue?
Soy una palabra.

Estoy como estás

Estoy como estás.
Confusión, claridad por instantes,
alegría fugaz
y eterna,
amargo odio odiado que sale.

Estoy como estás.
Un sordo que grita
su llanto sordo
que cae en cabezas
sin oídos y sin ojos.

La voz sale por los ojos
y la mano oye y suelta gritos
y los dedos se hablan y se acarician
y ríen.

Sin ojos, sin oídos,
la boca arrugada
cerrada sin moverse,
firme.
Nunca se abrirá,
no siente, no ve, no oye.
Solos los dedos, los dedos
y las manos,
las manos,
y el estómago que se mastica.

Estoy como estás.
Confusión, claridad por instantes
alegría fugaz
y eterna
amargo adiós odiado que sale.

Estoy como estás
un sordo que grita
su llanto sordo
que cae en cabezas
sin oídos y sin ojos.

La voz sale por los ojos
y la mano oye y suelta gritos
y los dedos se hablan y se acarician
y ríen.

Sin ojos, sin oídos.
La boca arrugada
cerrada sin moverse
firme.
nunca se abrirá
no siente, no ve, no oye,

Solos los dedos, los dedos
y las manos,
las manos.

Y el estómago que mastica

La vida por fin empezó

La vida por fin empezó
Salió del pasado, muerta.
La busqué años
      en sueños de esperanzas
      en vida eterna
      en muerte viva.

La encontré, la comprendo ya
      ahora nos vemos alegres
      ahora me sonríe cuando quiero
      ahora la cojo y la suelto, juego con ella
      ahora sé lo que es.

La puedo masticar y escupirla
      o comérmela
      o desearla
      o soñarla.

La vida la tengo en mis manos
      se mueve, se quiere saltar
      ahora me teme, la hice que saltara
      del pasado y por eso no me quiere a veces
      ahora me río de ella, ¡qué incapacitada
      está! Ahora es mi juguete.

Ahora que he encontrado mi vida buscaré otras.
Ahora puedo despegarme de ella, pegarme a otras.
Salió del pasado muerta, y por estar muerta
La comprendo, no la temo, no puede hacerme nada.

Finally Life Began

Finally life began
It came out of the past. Dead.
I searched years
    in dreams of hope
    in eternal life
    in living death.

Now I see and understand it
    now we see each other gladly at times
    now it laughs with me when I want it
    now I grab it and I play with it
    I know what it is.

I can chew it and spit it out
    or I can eat it
    or desire it
    or dream it.

I truly have life in my palms
    it moves, and wants to go free
    now it fears me
    I made it burst out of the past.
    How powerless it is. My toy.

Now I can detach myself from it
and attach myself to others.
It came out of the past. Dead.
Because it's dead I understand it.
I do not fear it.
It can do nothing to me.

To Walk Beyond the Door

To walk beyond the door
each day
out the door of eyes
To the right. To the left.
Straight ahead
directly in front
understood by everyone
out of the many
millions
waiting behind the door
yet unrecognized.
To walk beyond the reach
of eyes
beyond the door of doors
the ultimate one
the one at the very end
which encloses nothing
beyond here and there.

Another Day

Another day
yet not
for faces are the same
always
to be blind
would it matter?
Another day
feeling another day

I can see the sky moving
and the clouds turn
from purple
to red
to white
to blue
constantly colors

Left myself yesterday
encounter myself today
as I step into my face
and into my eyes

I see myself
yet in another day
really another yesterday

Not Unlike the Wind

Not unlike the wind
breathing eternally
into itself.

Not unlike the wind
who swallows
forever.

Moving
everything

You are through
the wind
a mystery.

A Flower

A flower
twitching
between lives
no, not of quiet desperation
between lives
unruly
to twitch
living
thinking
a flower
having captured time
and color
sure of itself
yet trembling
at the onlooker
will he kill
a flower
having captured the warm sun
also
and the many waves of
heat and sound
and my eyes.

Soy una palabra

Soy una palabra
Seré una palabra

En esta hoja,
aquí.

Te sigo desde aquí.

Espero,
siempre espero

el secreto eterno
contigo.

Soy una palabra.

Fake or Fink

I know this jovial man
Who stomps the ground and shouts "hurray"
When there are people in sight

I know this happy man
Who says "hello" and dresses well
When there are people in sight.

I know this Christian man
Who goes to church and pays his tithe
When there are people in sight.

I know this educated man
Who speaks so well and listens light
When there are people in sight

I know this wealthy man
Who shows his generosity and glistens his teeth
When there are people in sight.

I know this wealthy, educated, jovial, happy,
Christian man
Who cries and fears at night
Because he cannot do it
When there are people in sight.

Eternity

The living
live because of the dead,
and the dead lived
because of the dead.

And the living
will live dead
for the living.

The living will always be dead
and the dead will
always be living.

Eternity

The living
live because of the dead,
and the dead lived
because of the dead.

And the living
will live dead
for the living

The living will always be dead
and the dead will
  always be living

I Go to Church at 'Veteran's Place'

Go to church on Sunday and be saved,
Pray for us sinners.

I'll see you at one at *Veteran's Place*.
Where the German parachute and the machine gun
Will be looking at me.
The pictures on the wall
All those men in uniform will be looking at me.

And so will the luger and the Japanese flag
And so will the saber and the pliers with which
He handles hot checks.
Even Eisenhower will look at me,
Even General Pershing and his horse will be there.

The one-eyed empty beer bottles
Will look into my eyes and burp.

All those young men in uniform,
All those memories,
We must let them see us.

". . . for they have not died in vain"

Pray "for us sinners" on Sunday,
While we dance for the pictures
And the sorrowful jukebox.

Desátate

Soy del otro mundo y de éste.
¿De dónde eres tú?
¿Acaso eres de aquel nudo
que no pudo desatarse,
que dejó matarse?

Soy del otro mundo y de éste
porque me desaté.

¿Qué te cuesta? Piensa hombre ...
desátate, que eres inmortal mientras vives,
¿o es que no vives?

Eres el mundo, no eres mudo ... piensa
agita, haz, muévete, que estás vivo.
Desátate de ese nudo
o queda mudo y mortal viviente.

Soy del otro mundo y de éste
porque me desaté.

From the Past

From the past
from the past,
dead.
Search, search, in
the past.
Search, search, in
the future.
Yet, lingering in their presence.
Thread, upon thread, upon thread
mucus membrane
Is this all?
From the past
in the future
yet lingering
thread, upon thread, upon thread.

Through the Window

Alive,
swaying,
clinging,

drops.

Verge
transparently transparent
in concave
convex forms.

Life drops,
swaying drops,
drying.

Dry ring.

We Didn't Bury Him

We didn't bury him, they did.
They didn't know
That he had a ring with an M nor did they know
That he always brought pan dulce home.
That he never went to church but believed in
    God.
That he loved mother but had a mistress.
That he loved us but never touched us.
That he gave and worked but was avaricious.
That he cursed in English but not in Spanish.
That he drank and smoked once.

They didn't know that he kicked me once when
    I lost 10 cents.
And that he cried when his father died.

They didn't know that he taught me to cry.
And that he told me I was stupid when I cut my
    foot.

They didn't know that he baked the turkey at the
    wedding.
And that he winked his eye when we left on our
    honeymoon.
Nor did they know that he kissed our little girl
    when we
Were not looking.

They didn't know him, they buried him when he
    died.

We didn't. (I, my mother and brothers.)

My Life

A learned man spoke last night
Of the wonders and terrors of the world
Of how to live right
Of how not to live wrong
He talked and talked and made me happy for a
     while.

And then he was gone,
And I was alone
In the wonders of terrors of the world
And I was sadly happy.

And I understood
That I was truly alone, forever more alone,
That I had my own terrrors and wonders.
He had seen and known.

Now
I have to see and know the wonders and terrors
     of my life.

La luz

La luz
y el viento se elevan
a una altura y así levantan
cada vez más una etapa de conocimiento
cada vez más ajeno, más distante, más áspero
y mientras
yo no puedo meterme
en esa luz, en ese viento, en ese conocimiento
porque sólo puedo hablar desde
este nivel
desde este espacio
que respiro
y que soy
a lo menos hoy
nadamás

la luz
y el viento se elevan
a una altura y así levantan
cada vez más una etapa de conocimiento
cada vez más ajeno, más distante, más aspero
y mientras
yo no puedo meterme
en esa luz en ese viento, en ese conocimiento
porque solo puedo hablar desde
este nivel
desde este espacio
que es respiro
que vivo
y que soy
a lo menos hoy
nada más

Bibliography

Abbreviations:

AL   *Alaluz, Revista de poesía y narración* 12.1 (1980): 80.

AML   *We Are Chicanos: An Anthology of Mexican-American Literature.* Philip D. Ortego, ed. New York: Washington Square Press, 1973: 184-87.

AOP   *Always and Other Poems.* Sisterdale, TX: Sisterdale Press, 1973.

CS   *Cafe Solo* 8 (1974): 31-32.

EG   *El Grito* 3.1 (1969): 56-63.

ES   *El espejo/The Mirror.* Octavio Romano-V. and Herminio Ríos C., eds. Berkeley, CA: Quinto Sol, 1972, 2nd edition: 237-44. Reprint of *EG*.

ET   *English in Texas* (Texas Joint Council of Teachers of English) 10.2 (1978): 33, 35.

EL   *Ethnic Literatures since 1776: The Many Voices of America. Proceedings of the Comparative Literature Symposium 9,* Vol. I. Wolodymyr T. Zyla & Wendell M. Aycock, eds. Lubbock: Texas Tech Press, 1976: 27-31.

FLQ   *Original Works, A Foreign Language Quarterly* (Norman, OK: 1967): 10.

NB   *The New Breed: An Anthology of Texas Poets.* David Oliphant, ed. Malta, IL: Prickly Pear Press: 1973: 138-43.

QE   *El Quetzal Emplumece.* Carmela Montalvo, Leonardo Anguiano & Cecilio García-Camarillo, eds. San Antonio, TX: Mexican American Culture Center, 1976: 246-53.

RCR   *Revista Chicano-Riqueña* 1.1 (1973): 17-18.

SD   *Songs and Dreams.* Joseph A. Flores, ed. West Haven, CT: Pendulum Press, 1972: 80.

A Blas de Otero: *AL*
Alone: *CS*
A Most Tired Word: *AL/QE*
Another Me: *AL*
Always: *AL/CS*
Autumn and Winter: *AL*
Child, The: *ET/RCR*
De niño, De joven, De viejo: *EE/EG/QE*
Ennui: *AL*
Eyes of a Child, The: *AML*
Hide the Old People or American Idearium: *EE/EG/QE*
Me lo enterraron: *EE/EG/FLQ/QE*
M'ijo no mira nada: *EE/EG/QE*
Overalls, The: *AL/CS/NB*
Odio: *EE/EG/QE*
Past Possessions: *AL/AML*
Perfection of Perfections: *AL*
Poetics: *NB*
Rooster Crows en Iowa y en Texas, The: *EE/EG/ET/NB/QE*
Run, Puff, Run, Run: *AL/QE*
Searchers, The: *EL*
Seeds in the Hour of Seeds: *AL*
Siempre el domingo: *EE/EG/NB/QE*
Soundless Words: *AL/AML/CS/QE*
This Solitude: *AL/QE*
When Love To Be: *AML/ET/RCR*
Young Voices: *AL/ET/RCR/SD*

Chronology

I.   1967: "Me lo enterraron"

II. 1967-69:

    A. *El Grito*

        "De niño, de Joven, de viejo"
        "Hide the Old People, or American Idearium"
        "M'ijo no mira nada"
        "Odio"
        "The Rooster Crows en Iowa y en Texas"
        "Siempre el Domingo"

    B. From the same typescript containing the above are the following unpublished poems:

        "El despertar"
        "En la hora de las semillas"
        "Las voces del olvido"
        "Nacimiento"
        "Soy una palabra"

    C. Four-page typescript, unpublished:

        1. "Do Not Forget Me"
        2. "You Have Seen Me"
        3. "Love Seeds"
        4. "Window"
        Each page of this typescript of group C bears the autograph:

                1 of 4
                Tomás Rivera
                541 Sooner
                Norman, Okla.

Rivera lived at this address between 1967-69. Numbers 2-4 are primitive drafts of "Always," "Young Voices" and "Through the Window," respectively.

D.   "We Didn't Bury Him," translation of "Me lo enterraron."

E.   Among Rivera's literary documents, in the Tomás Rivera Archives, there are three autograph indices of his poetry. The one that appears to be the oldest lists most of the above poems and includes titles or primitive titles of poems subsequently published in *AML, AOP, CS* and *RCR*:

"Alone," *CS*

"Past Possessions," *AOP*

"Reach Beyond the Eyes of A Child" ("The Child"), *RCR*

"Run, Puff, Run, Run," *AOP*

"Seeds in the Hour of Seeds," *AOP*

"Solitude" ("This Solitude"), *AOP*

"Soundless Words," *AOP*

"The Word Is Tired ("A Most Tired Word"), *AOP*

"Things" ("Ennui"), *AOP*

"Young Voices," *RCR*

F.   The same index contains the following poems which remained unpublished:

"Desátate"

"Estoy como estás"

"Fake or Fink"

"Finally Life Began"

"My Life"

"Palabras" (under the primitive title of "En esta hoja blanca")

"[I Go to Church at] Veteran's Place"

"La vida por fin empezó" is not listed, but examination indicates that it was written before its translation, "Finally Life Began."

III. March 1968: "Palabras"; dated autograph.

IV. 1969-1972:

A. *Revista Chicano-Riqueña* (Spring, 1973):

"The Child"
"When Love To Be"
"Young Voices"

B. Group A was selected from a group of poems that Rivera submitted to *RCR*, and some of which remained unpublished:

"A Flower"
"Another Day"
"Not Unlike the Wind"
"Through the Window"

C. Groups A and B were selected from a typescript that includes the unpublished poems:

"Awakening" (trans. of "Nacimiento," II. 1967-69, B.)
"To Walk Beyond the Door"
and poems published in *AOP* (1973): "Always," "Another Me," "Perfection of Perfections."

D. *Always and Other Poems* (1973)

"A Most Tired Word," (II. 1967-69, E.)

"Always"

"Another Me"

"Autumn and Winter"

"Ennui," (II. 1967-69, E.)

"The Overalls"

"Past Possessions" (II. 1967-69, E.)

"Perfection of Perfections"

"Run, Puff, Run, Run" (II. 1967-69, E.)

"Seeds in the Hour of Seeds" (II. 1967-69, E.)

"Soundless Words" (II. 1967-69, E.)

"This Solitude" (II. 1967-69, E.)

"Young Voices"

    E.   "The Eyes of a Child" (*AML*, II. 1967-69, E.)

V. By 1976: "The Searchers," *Ethnic Literatures Since 1776*.

VI. Dec. 11, 1975: "Searching at Leal Middle School," dated typescript.

VII. 1979-80: "A Blas de Otero," *AL* (Blas de Otero: † 1979).

VIII. With the exception of specifically dated poems, all other poetry in Part II was probably written between 1967-72.

Notes to the Poems

De niño, de joven, de viejo

EG, ES: l. 36: "Los pasos cauteles" appears to include an erratum. The line should read: "Los pasos cautos" or "Los pasos cautelosos." Ll. 42-43: "Las miradas abajo / pensadas sentencias." "abajo" does not appear to be a preposition introducing "pensadas sentencias," in which case it would be "bajo" or "debajo de" as is the case with the preposition "detrás [de]" (l. 44). It is clearly an adverb, with "pensadas sentencias" in apposition to "las miradas abajo." Following the pattern established in the rest of the poem (e.g. ll. 40-41: "La ventana cerrada. / La mañana caliente . . . " and ll. 62-63: "Los sueños pasados, / los viejos amigos,") and to avoid confusion, I insert a comma: "las miradas abajo, / pensadas sentencias."

M'ijo no mira nada

In the typescript of II. A (see Chronology), this poem has a variant of the same poem published in El Grito. Line 6 of the published version has the child responding in Spanish: "¿Por qué pelea?," whereas his other responses to his father are in English. The variant gives for the same line: "Why does he fight?" While we cannot know the reasons why Rivera chose the published version, thematically and structurally it would seem that the variant given would have been the more appropriate. On one level, the poem deals with the linguistic and cultural alienation that can occur between Spanish-speaking parents and their children who choose not to retain or speak Spanish and seek assimilation into the English-speaking majority society. The unpublished version would have emphasized this cultural and linguistic drifting.

Seeds in the Hour of Seeds

Cf.: "Bartolo always came through town around December, when he felt that most of the people had returned from work in other states. He always sold his poems. They were almost completely sold out by the end of the first day because they mentioned the names of the people in town. And when he read the poems out loud, it was a serious and emotional experience. I remember once he told the people to read his poems out loud because the voice was the love seed in the dark," *Tierra*.

Young Voices

There are two primitive versions of this poem; one is "Love Seeds" (II.C.3) and the other, earlier, has a Spanish title, "la voz," although the text is in English. The most significant variant in the latter is the line between the third and fourth stanzas, which Rivera eliminated in his second draft:

REMEMBER , CHICANO,

the voice
is the love seed
in the dark

The Overalls

CS, NB, l. 9: "and the sound of clods"; CS, ll. 17-18: "the crushing / vapor"

Alone

A primitive version of this poem has three lines which Rivera eliminated from the conclusion of his final draft: "yet, they only remind me / that I am alone / forever"

A Blas de Otero

AL: ll. 1-2 present some confusion to the reader. As published in AL, the first word of the initial line begins in lower case, "la cicatriz del pecado original / Anonada la justicia y" (sic) The first word of the second line, corrected in this edition as "Anonadada," begins in upper case, as does the first word of the second and third stanzas, which seems to indicate that the word beginning in upper case introduces a stanza. The first line, "la cicatriz del pecado original," repeated in l. 21, may have been intended to function as an epigraph; at least it expresses a concept— reflecting the religious crisis of Otero's first books—which the rest of the poem glosses, comments or elucidates. In this regard, then, for this edition I have commenced the first line in upper case and have closed it with a colon, "La cicatriz del pecado original:"

The Searchers

I:12-15, 21-24 are popular children's rhymes found in Mexican/Chicano culture. "naranja dulce . . . que yo te pido": "sweet orange / a lemon cut / your embrace / is all I crave" "A la víbora . . . por aquí pueden pasar": "Oh, the serpent, serpent / of the sea / of the sea / through here you [children] may pass."

I:38, "Hay, ese vato, chíngate": "Hey, guy, go to hell."

I: 39, "terrón": clod of dirt.

II: 10-12, "Tierra eres . . . volverás": "Dust you are / dust you will be / and to dust you will return."

II:13-24, "Una noche caminando . . . alumbran allí": "One night walk-ing / a dark shade I saw / I withdrew from her / and she drew close to me. / What are you doing, sir? / What are you about here? / I am searching for my wife / who has been lost to me. / Your wife is no longer here, / your wife is now dead; / four candles white / are burning over there."

IV:32, "No estamos solos": "We are not alone."

VI:40, 42, "Pan dulce": sweet bread, pastry.

Searching at Leal Middle School

ll. 54-70, "Away in the dump yards . . . and magazines": "There is one book which especially impressed me: *In Darkest Africa* by Henry M. Stanley. I found it myself in the dump, you see; a two-volume collec-tion of Stanley's expedition into Africa in search of Dr. Livingstone. Of course, I didn't know anything about history at the time, or the explo-ration of Africa, but with the books came maps of the terrain through which Stanley had to travel. The text was a diary, a day-by-day account of what to Stanley was the discovery of Africa, with all the details, like how much food they ate, how far they had traveled, all those things. It fascinated me. It was better than going to a Tarzan movie. It carried over into my own life, because I started making maps of the terrain we traveled, and my brothers and I would explore and draw maps. It be-came a living thing. I haven't read them for a long time, but that title stuck in my memory because of the exploratory aspect . . . I still have those books at home . . . That was back in 1944; I was about nine," Bruce-Novoa, *Inquiry* 143; see "Notes to the Introduction," note 5.

Rivera sent a copy of this poem to a student at Leal Middle School, stating in a cover letter: "I really enjoyed participating with you and the other students at Leal Middle School yesterday. Many of you are interested in poetry writing, reading and reciting. Keep up the inter-est. The study of literature and the reading of literature, as you now know, is one of my greatest interests. It is so because it reveals original elements that we all have as people. After I talked to the three groups of students at Leal Middle School, I came back to my office and wrote the following poem which I titled *Leal Middle School*. I have attached it here"(December 18, 1975).

Finally Life Began

Rivera does not translate one line from the Spanish version, the first of the final stanza, which would be: "Now that I've found my life, I'll search for others."

Through the Window

There are two primitive versions; the one that appears to be the earliest, an autograph, is titled "Life drops,"while the second draft, typed, is titled by hand, "Window," above the struck typed title of "Reincarnation." This version has a concluding line, eliminated in the final version, of a single word: "Death."

Notes to the Introduction

[1]Tomás Rivera, ... *y no se lo tragó la tierra/ ... and the earth did not part*, Herminio Ríos and Octavio I. Romano-V., trans. (Berkeley: Quinto Sol Publications, Inc. 1971); ... *y no se lo tragó la tierra/ ... and the earth did not devour him*, Evangelina Vigil-Piñón, trans. (Houston: Arte Publico Press, 1987).

[2]Tomás Rivera, *The Harvest, Short Stories/La cosecha, cuentos*, Julián Olivares, ed. (Houston: Arte Publico Press, 1989).

[3]Tomás Rivera, "Into the Labyrinth: The Chicano in Literature," *New Voices in Literature: The Mexican American, A Symposium* (Edinburg, TX: Pan American University, 1971): 18.

[4]Tomás Rivera, "Chicano Literature: Fiesta of the Living," *Books Abroad* 49.3 (1975): 439. Rivera's concept of the 'other'—"the 'other' is the bosom of reason itself, as the object of the sentimental and instinctive ego, as the moral activity of the ego, as found in the dialectics of the subjective spirit and the dialectics of nature, as an invention of the ego, as phenomenological reflection"—is taken from Pedro Laín Entralgo, *Teoría y realidad del otro* (note to "Fiesta" 439). See also, Tomás Rivera, "Recuerdo, descubrimiento y voluntad en el proceso imaginativo literario"/"Remembering, Discovery and Volition in the Literary Imaginative Process," *Atisbos, Journal of Chicano Research* 1 (1975): 66-76.

[5]See Bruce-Novoa, "Tomás Rivera," *Chicano Authors: Inquiry by Interview* (Austin: University of Texas Press, 1980): 140-41.

[6]In researching Rivera's unpublished poetry and in preparing this edition, I have sometimes felt as if I were possibly publishing some poems that Rivera may have wanted to discard, as if I were searching through his wastebasket (an act of discovery in his refuse?). Those poems, some incomplete and some drafts, that I do not include in this collection and which I wish to document are:

"Blankness and Darkness"
"Shoes Thump"
"For Rhonda Burnam"
"In the Park"
"To err is human, to forgive divine"
"Lack of Symbols"
"The Fibre Content"
Untitled, first line: "That building is called a skyscraper. It is very tall."

Untitled, first line: "She goes to communion every Sunday and confesses every Saturday."

Untitled, first line: "You will now forget the past."

[7]For a fuller discussion of "The Searchers" and for an introduction to . . . *y no se lo tragó la tierra*, see my "The Search for Being, Identity and Form in the Work of Tomás Rivera," *International Studies in Honor of Tomás Rivera*, Julián Olivares, ed. (Houston: Arte Publico Press, 1986 [*Revista Chicano-Riqueña* 13.3-4 (1985)]: 66-80; see also the other articles in this *festschrift*.

[8]For the translation of the Spanish text in "The Searchers," see the "Notes to Poems."

[9]For Rivera's incorporation of folklore models and motifs, see Nicolás Kanellos, "Language and Dialog in . . . *y no se lo tragó la tierra*," in *International Studies in Honor of Tomás Rivera*: 53-65; and the "Introduction" of *The Harvest*; see also Rivera's "Chicano Literature: Fiesta of the Living."

[10]"What I remember most about that night was the darkness, the mud and the slime of the salamanders, and how hard they would get when I tried to squeeze the life out of them. What I have with me still is what I saw and felt when I killed the last one, and I guess that is why I remember the night of the salamanders. I caught one and examined it very carefully under the lamp. Then I looked at its eyes for a long time before I killed it. What I saw and what I felt is something I still have with me, something that is very pure—original death," "The Salamanders," *The Harvest*, 90.